IMAGES
of America

WEST ROXBURY

The Charles River at the Spring Street Bridge was the scene of canoeists at the turn of the century. On the right is the boathouse of the Samoset Canoe Club and their canoe livery. (Courtesy of the West Roxbury Historical Society.)

IMAGES
of America

WEST ROXBURY

Anthony Mitchell Sammarco

ARCADIA

First published 1997
Copyright © Anthony Mitchell Sammarco, 1997

ISBN 0-7524-0452-0

Published by Arcadia Publishing,
an imprint of the Chalford Publishing Corporation,
One Washington Center, Dover, New Hampshire 03820.
Printed in Great Britain

Library of Congress Cataloging-in-Publication Data applied for

John Sawtell Smiley and his horse Dandy pose on Vermont Street for this photograph in 1910.
(Courtesy of the West Roxbury Historical Society.)

Contents

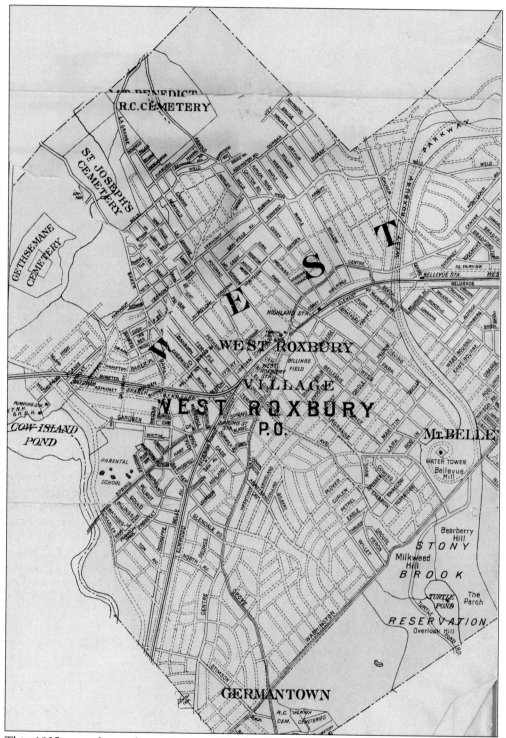

This 1905 map shows the various neighborhoods in West Roxbury, which include West Roxbury Village, Germantown, and Mount Bellevue. (Courtesy of Stephen D. Paine.)

Introduction

West Roxbury has existed as a neighborhood of Boston since its annexation to the city in 1874. In the seventeenth century, the town was a part of Roxbury, Massachusetts, which had been settled by the Puritans in 1630, and extended from the present town to the border of Dedham, Massachusetts. The area was then referred to as "Spring Street" or as the "Jamaica End" of Roxbury.

In the first years of the American Revolution, residents of the Spring Street area of Roxbury petitioned the Massachusetts General Court to set themselves off from Roxbury and incorporate themselves as the town of "Washington," in honor of General George Washington (1732–1799) who commanded the American troops. However, the petition fell on deaf ears and the separatists' voices were not heard again until the early 1850s, when their cries for independence resulted in the granting of their ardent wishes. On May 24, 1851, the western section of Roxbury was set off and incorporated as the independent town of West Roxbury. The new town included present-day West Roxbury as well as Roslindale and Jamaica Plain, and town meetings alternated between Taft's Tavern in Roslindale Village and the village hall on Thomas Street, in present-day Jamaica Plain, for "the greatest convenience of the greatest number" of residents.

West Roxbury in the nineteenth century was a rural section of the countryside, with mostly farmers living on vast tracts of land. This rural aspect is what drew Reverend George Ripley when he established the Brook Farm Institute of Agriculture and Education on September 29, 1841. A utopian community, Brook Farm's purpose was "more effectually to promote the great purposes of human culture; to establish the external relations of life on a basis of wisdom and purity; to apply the principles of justice and love to our social organization . . .; to establish a system of brotherly cooperation for one of selfish competition; to secure to our children and those who may be entrusted to our care the benefits of the highest physical, intellectual and moral education in the present state of human knowledge that the resources at our command will permit; to institute an attractive, efficient and productive system of industry; to prevent the exercise of worldly anxiety by the competent supply of our necessary wants; to diminish the desire of excessive accumulation by making the acquisition of individual property subservient to upright and disinterested uses; to guarantee to each other the means of physical support and of spiritual progress and thus to impart a greater freedom, simplicity, truthfulness, refinement and moral dignity to our mode of life." These lofty, and sincere, ideals would make Brook Farm and West Roxbury known throughout the world.

The West Roxbury Branch of the Boston and Providence Railroad was completed in 1848, fourteen years after the railroad was established, with stations at Central (later known as Bellevue), West Roxbury Village, and Spring Street. The town was comprised of three sections: West Roxbury Village, or what is now the Centre Street area; Mount Bellevue, which was literally named for the beautiful views afforded by the hill; and Germantown, a section near the junction of Washington and Grove Streets that was settled by Germans from East Dedham. It was said that in "1851, there were two churches, two grocery stores, and one small dry goods store, and for many years after conditions remained unchanged."

In fact, so sparsely was the town settled that the only streets that predated the Civil War were South and Centre Streets, Walter, Weld, Church, Willow, Spring, Baker, Beech, and Cottage Streets, and Lyons Lane (now Bellevue Street). The meetinghouse was located at the corner of

Centre and Church Streets and was known as the Second Church in Roxbury, founded in 1711. The parishioners built a larger meetinghouse in 1773, which served their needs until 1890. The early families who lived in West Roxbury and pursued farming are perpetuated in the names of streets; these streets recall the Draper, Corey, Colburn, Whiting, Richards, Billings, Chapin, and Weld families who were the early residents of the Spring Street area. However, by the mid-nineteenth century, new residents began moving to West Roxbury, as its rural charm and country setting, all within a short distance from Boston on the Dedham Branch railroad, proved an attraction. Large estates were developed in Forest Hills, the Baker Street area, and Cottage Avenue (now Saint Theresa Avenue).

However, it was the West Roxbury Branch of the railroad that brought the middle class to West Roxbury, and initiated the great changes that were to take place between 1860 and 1900. Though some of the estates remained well into the twentieth century—most notably the Codman Estate (later the campus of the Roxbury Latin School) and the Cabot Estate (the site of the present Saint Theresa's Church)—it would be the real estate developers who subdivided the farms and created new neighborhoods, thus transforming the once rural countryside into urban streetscapes that would become known as "Streetcar Suburbs." The close proximity of West Roxbury to Boston, with travel made easier by the railroad and the West Roxbury and Roslindale Street Railway, proved far too much of a temptation for the developers, and the push for annexation to the city of Boston became the primary topic of discussion. Boston had already annexed the once independent city of Roxbury (1867) and the town of Dorchester (1870), and the filling in of the marshlands west of Arlington Street in Boston had created the new "Back Bay" neighborhood, but the steadily increasing population continued to demand more space. Through the rapid transformation of West Roxbury into a suburb of Boston, it seemed that annexation was inevitable, and West Roxbury (along with the city of Charlestown and the town of Brighton) was annexed to Boston on May 29, 1873, with the annexation taking effect on January 5, 1874. Thus, the town of West Roxbury ceased to exist twenty-three years after it was founded, and now became a neighborhood of the city of Boston.

The resultant change in West Roxbury was swift and decisive. The opponents to the annexation saw their property soar in value and the proponents began the further subdivision of the farms and estates to attract new residents to the neighborhood. By the last decade of the nineteenth century, the population was served by a street railway line that operated between Forest Hills and Dedham. The Boston Elevated Railway had completed the elevated railway that connected Dudley Street in Roxbury to Sullivan Square in Charlestown in 1901. This line was extended to Forest Hills in 1909, and created a passenger terminus for the streetcars that connected Dedham along Spring and Grove Streets and Centre Street. With the increased ease of transportation, West Roxbury became a desirable and accessible neighborhood that would continue to increase steadily in population.

With the increase in population came new schools and churches, along with new streets and major roads, such as the Veterans of Foreign Wars Parkway. The housing boom took place initially in the 1920s and early 1930s, but would double after World War II, due in part to the automobile and to the Veterans Bill that allowed for low interest mortgages for veterans. Today, West Roxbury is a thriving neighborhood of Boston, with open space along the Charles River and Mount Bellevue. With a large number of cemeteries, such as the Saint Joseph's, Gethsemane, and Mount Benedict Cemeteries, and the Jewish cemeteries of Adath-Jeshurun, Baker Street, and Boston United Hand in Hand, the open space once so attractive to our ancestors remains, but perceived and utilized in a different manner.

Though Brook Farm was known throughout the world as an important utopian experiment, today West Roxbury is more than just the Brook Farm's former site. It is a thriving community of people, who strive to make it a pleasant and livable neighborhood that offers suburban living in the city. I hope that you enjoy this photographic history of the development of West Roxbury, which is poignantly shown in photographs from the collection of the West Roxbury Historical Society.

One
Early West Roxbury

A panorama of mid-nineteenth century West Roxbury is seen looking west from Park Street. Centre Street, a part of the Dedham Post Road, passes the Second Church of Roxbury on the far right, and houses and farms dot the hill that was later subdivided for Esther, Greaton, Manthorne, Garnet, and Redlands Roads, and Willow and Maple Streets. (Courtesy of the West Roxbury Historical Society.)

The Old Richard's Tavern was on Centre Street opposite the present library. Built in 1675, it later became the "ell" of the new tavern, built in the early nineteenth century. (Courtesy of the Boston Public Library, hereinafter referred to as the BPL.)

The Whiting Tavern was a famous inn on Centre Street, between Elgin and Temple Streets. This hipped roof colonial tavern dispensed hospitality from about 1760 until the mid-nineteenth century, and stages traveling from Boston to Providence often stopped here. The tavern was later owned by the Hay family, and was demolished in 1892. (Courtesy of the West Roxbury Historical Society.)

Richard's Tavern was built about 1675 on Centre Street. Nathaniel Richards, the inn keeper, once offered hospitality to General George Washington. Located on the present site of the West Roxbury Post Office, members of the Madden family, who purchased the inn in 1866, pose in 1880 on the lawn in front of the ancient inn. (Courtesy of the West Roxbury Historical Society.)

A panorama of West Roxbury is seen from the cupola of the Davidson family home on Willow Street in 1880. (Courtesy of the West Roxbury Historical Society.)

The Weld Farm was an extensive tract of land that was owned by one of Roxbury's oldest and most prominent families. The farmhouse, seen on the left, had extensive outbuildings. The hay barn with the cupola was in the center, and there were three horse barns and a coach barn on the right. The farmhouse was the home of the Welds until it was demolished in 1949. (Courtesy of the West Roxbury Historical Society.)

The "plough gate" was literally a gate composed of a plow, rake, pitchfork, hoe, and shovel that would be used by farm workers. The gate was on the Weld Farm on South Street in what is now Brookline, Massachusetts, and is perpetuated in the present "Plowgate Avenue." (Courtesy of the West Roxbury Historical Society.)

Horses drink from a spring on the Weld Farm at the turn of the century. (Courtesy of the West Roxbury Historical Society.)

A farmhand guides horses across South Street to a grazing field on the Weld Farm. (Courtesy of the West Roxbury Historical Society.)

Two gentlemen pose on Willow Lane, off Centre Street, in 1890, with the branches of mature willow trees arching above. (Courtesy of the West Roxbury Historical Society.)

Cass' Corner was the nineteenth-century appellation of the junction of Centre and Spring Streets. Cass Street, which presently joins both streets, perpetuates the name of the corner today. (Courtesy of the West Roxbury Historical Society.)

This mid-nineteenth century country scene was the junction of Beech Street and Anawan Avenue. Today, the West Roxbury Parkway passes through this once bucolic setting that had been the Farrington Farm. (Courtesy of the West Roxbury Historical Society.)

The Judson Chapin House was a colonial farmhouse on Centre Street at the junction of Chapin Avenue. (Courtesy of the West Roxbury Historical Society.)

The Benjamin Guild House was on Centre Street near La Grange Street. (Courtesy of the West Roxbury Historical Society.)

Looking down Centre Street in 1880, from the corner of Corey Street. Dr. Draper's house can be seen at the corner of Centre and Park Streets. The old blacksmith's shop of C.P. Martshorn is on the right; later the shop was moved across the street and became known as McKenna's Blacksmith Shop. (Courtesy of the West Roxbury Historical Society.)

Dr. Abijah Draper's house was at the corner of Centre and Park Streets. (Courtesy of the West Roxbury Historical Society.)

Dr. Abijah Weld Draper was known as "a kind, sympathetic friend in sickness, and a true friend in need." He was born in Roxbury (which later became West Roxbury), and followed his father's career as the only doctor between Dedham and Jamaica Plain. (Courtesy of the BPL.)

The Attwill House was a rambling mansion built by Edward and Rachel Davis Richards in 1799 on Centre Street. It is the present site of Roche Brothers' Market. (Courtesy of the West Roxbury Historical Society.)

The parlor of the Attwill House was a spacious and comfortable room containing three generations of the family's furniture and collections. (Courtesy of the West Roxbury Historical Society.)

Looking west on Centre Street, from the corner of La Grange Street in 1875. The Dana House can be seen through the trees. Notice the sign on the right advertising "Frost Bros. Livery Stall." (Courtesy of the West Roxbury Historical Society.)

The Samuel B. Dana House was a substantial Georgian colonial house on Centre Street, just west of La Grange Street. (Courtesy of the West Roxbury Historical Society.)

Francis Gould Shaw moved to West Roxbury from Boston and "was one of the busiest men in town, intensely interested in all living things, he only wanted to know what needed doing and it was done promptly." His son, Colonel Robert Gould Shaw, led the 54th Massachusetts Infantry during the Civil War.

Looking up Corey Street from Center Street in 1880. The Morse House was on the right and the Whittemore House on the left. (Courtesy of the West Roxbury Historical Society.)

A group of friends walk through the woods in 1903 at what is now the area of Lassell and Vermont Streets. (Courtesy of the West Roxbury Historical Society.)

Charles A. Hewins was a merchant who was "extremely fond of his land, beautifying it with anything he could get to accomplish that end." (Courtesy of the BPL.)

WEST ROXBURY.

Tune—"Dearest Mae!"

Ring—ring your bells, Jamaica, and ring with merry glee!
Ring—ring your bells, Jamaica,—you are from City free;
Bring out your girls, Jamaica—and let them merry be,
And let them dance and let them sing, beneath the greenwood tree.
Three cheers for Roxbury City—and our good friends below,
Who prayed to those who held the power,—*in peace to let us go.*
Three cheers for General Wilson,—and three for Speaker Banks—
Both in the fight stood by the right—they have our hearty thanks!

Ring—ring your bells, West Roxbury—and ring with merry glee!
Ring—ring your bells, West Roxbury—a township great and free;
Bring out your girls, West Roxbury—the fairest of the fair—
And let them dance, and let them sing, and breathe this freer air.
Six cheers for Captain Bassett—and Wellington the true—
Six cheers for Parks and Hathaway—they put our Charter through.

West Roxbury boys with bonfires—proclaim that you are free—
Let every hill and every dale reflect your liberty!
The Morning sun beheld you bound—the Evening sees you free,—
Then let the welkin sound with joy—and let all merry be.
Nine cheers for all our noble friends, who faithful proved and true—
Who for our right maintained the fight—maintained, and conquered too!

Saturday, May 24, 1851.

---

1. RALPH HASKINS, Esq., and twenty other gentlemen of high character at Roxbury City, made a forcible appeal to the Legislature, in behalf of the petitioners, asking " to let them go in peace." Honorable mention thereof should be made in the records of West Roxbury. Mr. Wilson, President of the Senate and Mr. Banks, Speaker of the House, heartily sympathised with the petitioners for division.

2. The Hon. Messrs Bassett and Wellington of the Senate, and Messrs Parks and Hathaway of the House, were the four gentlemen of the Committee, who joined in the majority report; they sustained the petitioners with great vigor and effect. West Roxbury gratefully appreciates their generous and hearty support.

On Saturday, May 24, 1851, West Roxbury officially separated from the city of Roxbury and celebrated with "great rejoicing, by the firing of cannon, bell ringing, speeches, and fireworks." West Roxbury was comprised of West Roxbury, Roslindale, and Jamaica Plain from 1851 until 1874, when it was annexed to Boston,. This broadside tune *West Roxbury* was sung in exultant jubilation! (Courtesy of the West Roxbury Historical Society.)

The Billings House was on Centre Street, just past La Grange Street. An Italianate house with a mansard roof, it had a carriage house on the left. (Courtesy of the West Roxbury Historical Society.)

Lemuel Billings was photographed in his carriage at the junction of Centre and South Streets in 1886. (Courtesy of the West Roxbury Historical Society.)

WELCOME HOME BY THE OLD LAGRANGE COR. GANG. 1919

The "Old La Grange Corner Gang" had a Welcome Home party for veterans of World War I in 1919. From left to right are: (front row) Oliver Wize, Earl Thompson, and veteran Charles O'Connell; (middle row) Red Murry, veteran Charles Feeney, veteran William Feeney, and Charles Conway; (back row) Roy Thompson, Jack Twombley, veteran Charles Craig, Leo Hennessy, Vincent Gilligan, and Frank Furlong. (Courtesy of the West Roxbury Historical Society.)

The Westerly Burying Ground on Centre Street, near La Grange Street, was laid out in 1685 as a burying ground for residents of the "Spring Street" area of Roxbury. Named to the National Register of Historic Places in 1986, it is maintained by the Historic Burying Ground Initiative of Boston. (Courtesy of the West Roxbury Historical Society.)

Westerly Burying Ground 1839

Two
Brook Farm

Brook Farm Institute of Agriculture and Education was an utopian community established in 1841 by Reverend George Ripley, former minister of the Purchase Street Unitarian Church in Boston. At the time of its founding, Brook Farm stood unique among the many experimental communities in the nineteenth century "in its liberal, free spirit, its tolerance and the mental and moral caliber of many of the men and women who had connection with it." On the far left is the "Pilgrim House," next the "Cottage," then the "Eyrie" on top of the knoll, and "The Hive" on the far right. (Courtesy of the West Roxbury Historical Society.)

Brook Farm was actually named for a brook that meandered its way west from the Charles River through the farm and then continued on to Newton. Ripley described the farm in glowing terms and said that "we might search the country in vain for anything more eligible." Today the brook is known as the "Brook Farm Brook."

Brook Farm had been the dairy farm of Charles Ellis until it was purchased by Reverend Ripley for the community. A herd of dairy cows was photographed in the 1930s near the brook.

Reverend George Ripley was the founder of the Brook Farm Institute of Agriculture and Education. In April of 1841, he moved to Brook Farm with his wife, Sophia Warren Dana Ripley, and his sister, Marianne Ripley. Brook Farm, which existed between 1841 and 1847, was a cooperative society and idealistic enterprise based on transcendentalism. It raised comment at the time and "has forever since been looked back to as a romantic day dream or a golden age."

The buildings at Brook Farm represented simple structures such as a common dining building, a school that was conducted in "The Nest," and the "Eyrie," the residence of the Ripleys. Shortly thereafter a greenhouse, print shop, and a britanniaware shop were built and "every member of the community was expected to participate in some such kind of practical activity, domestic service, agriculture and the like."

One of the prominent members of Brook Farm was Nathaniel Hawthorne, a noted author who recorded his experiences in his book *The Blithedale Romance*. Other well-known persons who often visited, but ironically never joined Brook Farm, included Horace Greeley, A. Bronson Alcott, Ralph Waldo Emerson, and Reverend Theodore Parker.

George William Curtis said of the lively vigor and intellectuality of the farm that "there were never such witty potato patches and sparking cornfields before or since." Curtis became the literary critic and editor of *Harper's Weekly* and *Harper's Easy Chair* after he left Brook Farm.

Dr. Orestes Augustus Brownson was a man who "had experienced so many kinds of religion before he 'walked backward into the Catholic Church' that it was once remarked of him, when a preacher invited to the communion table the members of all Christian churches, that Brownson was the only person in the congregation who could 'fill the bill.'"

Father Isaac Hecker became a Catholic priest after he left Brook Farm, and later founded the Paulist Order. It was said of him that his "mysticism was of that extreme type, and his thinking so deeply grounded itself in the emotional and visionary, that there could be but one result of his intense religious enthusiasm."

"The Nest" was the school at Brook Farm and was "established on principles of teaching much like those which now are described as Progressive Education. Pupils were received as boarders from New York and some Spanish boys were even sent as students from the Philippines." So erudite was the community that they published their own newspaper, *The Harbinger*.

John Sullivan Dwight was a noted musician who had "spent a brief period as the transcendentalist preacher to the Unitarian congregation in Northampton [Massachusetts], which proved by no means friendly to his special teachings." Dwight later married Miss Mary Bullard, one of the "sweet singers" who often visited Brook Farm.

Charles A. Dana was not only the treasurer of Brook Farm but the recording secretary; before he joined the community in 1841 he was a clerk in Buffalo and in later life he was the editor of the *New York Sun*.

Brook Farm went as far as to print its own paper currency. This note was known as *Brook Farm Phalanx* money, and was worth 5¢.

The Margaret Fuller Cottage was a small wood-framed cottage that was built by Mrs. Alvord, who only occupied it for a short period of time. Margaret Fuller never joined the utopian community, but often visited, staying at the cottage while visiting her brother Lloyd, who boarded at Brook Farm. In 1842 she gave a series of "conversations" there, which were alternated with corn-husking parties.

Margaret Fuller (1810–1850), later the Marchése Ossoli, was described by Hawthorne as having "a strong and coarse nature which she had done her utmost to refine with infinite pains . . . Margaret has not left in the hearts and minds of those who knew her any deep witness of her integrity and purity. She was a great humbug." Margaret, her husband, and her young son were killed in the wreck of the *Elizabeth* off the coast of New York on a trip from Italy.

32

Reverend Warren Burton was a graduate of Harvard College and Theological School. He was a classmate of Reverend Ripley, and was one of three ministers who joined Brook Farm.

Dr. John Codman wrote extensively of his experiences at Brook Farm in his fascinating book *Historic and Personal Memoirs of Brook Farm.*

The woods that surrounded Brook Farm were an enchanting place, much like those described in Hawthorne's *The Blithedale Romance*: "Often in these years that are darkening around me I remember our beautiful scheme of a noble and unselfish life; and how fair, in that first summer, appeared the prospect that it might endure for generations, and be perfected, as the ages rolled away, into the system of a people and a world!"

After Brook Farm failed, it was purchased in 1849 by the city of Roxbury as a Poor Farm, but it was later sold in 1855 to Reverend James Freeman Clarke. Clarke let it to the Commonwealth of Massachusetts during the Civil War, and Union soldiers camped here. The farm was later purchased in 1870 by Gottlieb F. Burkhardt, a wealthy beer brewer, who presented it to the Martin Luther Home, an orphanage for German children.

The Martin Luther Home for Orphans allowed the children to grow up in the country and to learn to be self-sufficient, as they assisted with growing produce and keeping a herd of dairy cattle.

The children at the Martin Luther Home look remarkably healthy in this turn-of-the-century photograph. The trustees of the home met monthly at the Evangelical Lutheran Trinity Chapel on Parker Street in Roxbury to oversee the direction of Burkhardt's generosity.

Orphans from the Martin Luther Home ride in a horse-drawn wagon at the turn of the century.

By the beginning of the twentieth century, the land of the former Brook Farm was used not only by the Martin Luther Home but also as Gethsemane Cemetery, which had been laid out in the center of the farm. The drive to Brook Farm, off Baker Street, was photographed about 1915, showing how rural the area remained during the early twentieth century.

Three
Places of Worship

The Second Church of Christ in Roxbury was founded in 1711, after having petitioned the Roxbury Meeting House for leave to erect a meetinghouse in the Peter's Hill area of the western section of Roxbury, Massachusetts. The first minister was Reverend Ebenezer Thayer, and the original meetinghouse was used until 1773, when this meetinghouse was built farther south on Centre Street at the corner of Church Street. Photographed about 1875, the church was used until 1890, when it was damaged by fire. (Courtesy of the BPL.)

The Second Church of Roxbury was a simple white meetinghouse that had a spire added in 1821. The church had a bell that was cast in 1827 in East Medway, Massachusetts, and was rung every Fourth of July to mark Independence Day. By the mid-nineteenth century the church had become a thriving parish.

Reverend Theodore Parker served as minister of the Second Church of Roxbury from 1837 to 1846. Parker entered Harvard College when he was twenty years of age and graduated in 1836 from the theological course. An ardent abolitionist, as well as a prolific writer, he was respected, if not loved, by his parishioners and neighbors alike.

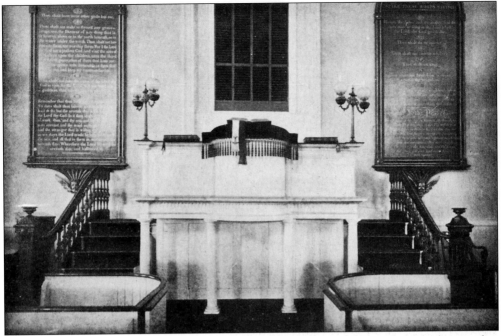

The pulpit of the Second Church was impressive, with lamps on either side of the lectern that held the Bible. (Courtesy of the BPL.)

The gallery extended on three sides of the meetinghouse and had an organ above the center entrance. The gallery clock, made by Simon Willard of Roxbury, was "Presented to the Second Church in Roxbury by Samuel Cookson, Esq.," as inscribed on the dial of the clock. (Courtesy of the BPL.)

Centre Street was intersected by Church Street on the right and South Street on the left. This 1880 photograph shows an unpaved Centre Street rutted by the marks of carriage wheels. (Courtesy of the West Roxbury Historical Society.)

Theodore Parker lived in this Federal house on Centre Street while minister of the Second Church of Roxbury. It was once the home of "I. Sylvan, enemy of human diseases,"; known locally as the rainwater doctor, his residence was quite brief, as the community did not stand for his medical quackery. Three friends walk past the house at the turn of the century. (Courtesy of David Rooney.)

Reverend Dexter Clapp was minister of the Second Church of Roxbury from 1848 to 1851. Though only settled for a short period of time, he won the respect of his parishioners, for he "loved to ramble about the woods and fields; nothing pleased him more than to go into a field and take a plough by the handles and tell how he used to work about the farm when a boy." (Courtesy of the BPL.)

The Second Church of Roxbury built this comfortable Italianate house as a parsonage, which was used as such from 1847 to 1889. The Rooney family later purchased it and lived here until the house was acquired as the rectory of Holy Name Church. The church used it until 1934, when the present rectory was built. (Courtesy of the BPL.)

The Second Church in Roxbury built a new church at the corner of Centre and Corey Streets in 1890. Designed by Alexander Wadsworth Longfellow of the architectural firm of Longfellow, Alden and Harlow, this part of the church is now used as the parish house and community center. (Courtesy of the BPL.)

The nave of the 1890 church was a simple space with wood trussing supporting the roof. It remained in use until 1900. (Courtesy of the BPL.)

The Second Church of Roxbury voted to rename their new church the Theodore Parker Church, in memory of the forthright and beloved minister of the church. Parker had penned the following prayer which shows his depth of perception:

"Father, I will not ask for wealth or fame,
Though once they would have joyed my carnal sense;
I shudder not to bear a hated name,
Wanting all wealth, myself my sole defence.
But give me, Lord, eyes to behold the truth;
A seeing sense that knows the eternal right;
A heart with pity filled, and gentlest ruth;
A manly faith that makes all darkness light.
Give me the power to labor for mankind;
Make me the mouth of such as cannot speak;
Eyes let me be to groping men and blind;
A conscience to the base; and to the weak
Let me be hands and feet; and to the foolish, mind;
And let furthur on such as thy kingdom seek."

The Theodore Parker Church, originally known as the First Parish, Unitarian, in West Roxbury, was designed by Henry Seaver as a harmonious extension of the present church, with rough hewn granite blocks and a crenelated bell tower. The church was further embellished with seven stained-glass memorial windows by Louis Comfort Tiffany and Tiffany Studios which were installed between 1894 and 1927. The church has been designated a Boston Landmark (in 1985) and a National Registered Landmark.

The nave of the new church was impressive and spacious with wood-framed timberwork on the ceiling, dark oak pews, and Tiffany windows. The cornerstone of the new church was laid on November 21, 1899, and the dedication of the church took place on October 5, 1900. (Courtesy of the BPL.)

A bronze statue of Theodore Parker, sculpted by Robert Kraus, was placed on a granite plinth base in front of the church on Centre Street in 1902. The public subscribed to the statue, which had been intended as an ornament for the Boston Public Garden, but the Boston Art Commission "thought it was not a good likeness," and it was stored until 1902. Bronze tablets on the sides of the base commemorate Parker's life and accomplishments.

The Old South Evangelical Church was an impressive Greek Revival church with a belfry that had a four-sided clock; it stood adjacent to the Mount Vernon Street School, seen on the left at the corner of Centre and Mount Vernon Streets. The church was founded in 1835 as the Spring Street Parish, with Reverend Christopher Marsh as the first pastor. (Courtesy of the West Roxbury Historical Society.)

The West Roxbury Congregational Church was a large Shingle-style church built on the site of the Old South Evangelical Church, at the corner of Centre and Mount Vernon Streets. It was adjacent to Westerly Hall, seen on the right. A "horseless carriage" passes the church, seen here about 1910.

The West Roxbury Congregational Church was built in 1891, on the site of the Old South Evangelical Church on Centre Street. The new addition to the West Roxbury Branch of the Boston Public Library now occupies the site.

On Independence Day in 1894 the altar of the West Roxbury Congregational Church was bedecked with American flags and ivy-covered portraits of President Ulysses Simpson Grant (on the left) and President Abraham Lincoln. (Courtesy of the West Roxbury Historical Society.)

Emmanuel Church was built at the corner of Stratford Street and Clement Avenue in 1893, on land donated for the church by Mr. William B. Blakemore, a local real estate developer. The building was designed by Reverend H.G. Wood as a stone structure seating about three hundred people. J. Lawrence Berry designed the parish house.

Emmanuel Church had been founded at a meeting in Highland Hall in 1892, and the first rector was Reverend William Osgood Pearson. Pearson was succeeded by Reverend Samuel Snelling in 1900. Though it had a small congregation, the "parish has been especially remarkable for the good work accomplished by its guilds and societies."

The Wesley Memorial Methodist Episcopal Church was designed by Boston architect Oscar A. Thayer and was built in 1890 on Park Street. A wood shingle-and-timber-framed church, it is now Saint Matthew's Syrian Orthodox Church.

The Riverdale Congregational Church was a small brick chapel with exaggerated rustication around the lancet door, circular window, and corner quoining. (Courtesy of the West Roxbury Historical Society.)

Saint Theresa's Church was built on Spring Street as a mission of Saint Mary's Church in Dedham, Massachusetts. After Sacred Heart Church was built in 1893 in Roslindale, Saint Theresa's was a mission of Sacred Heart until it was established as a separate parish.

Sitting on the front steps to Saint Theresa's Church on Spring Street at the turn of the century were the following, from left to right: (front row) Arthur Kane, an unidentified young man, Reverend Boyle, a Mission Father visiting Saint Theresa's, Joe Fallon, and George Parsons; (middle row) Thomas Shea, Tom Flynn, Fred Ferson, Frank McDonough, Waldo Hasenfus, and Harry Flynn; (back row) James Scanlon, Bob Kennedy, an unidentified young man, Andrew McKenna, and Frank Aberton. (Courtesy of the West Roxbury Historical Society.)

Shaded by a massive Elm tree, Saint Theresa's was a pleasant wood-framed church that served the steadily increasing Catholic population in West Roxbury. The present Saint Theresa of Avila Church at the corner of Centre Street and Cottage Avenue was built in 1930 from designs by the architectural firm of Maginnis and Walsh. (Courtesy of the West Roxbury Historical Society.)

Reverend Theodore Parker's former home at the corner of Centre Street and Cottage Avenue (now Saint Theresa Avenue) became the "parochial residence" of the priests serving at Saint Theresa's Church. It was later moved back when the present church was built, and demolished when the present rectory was built in 1955.

The parish of Holy Name Church was established in 1927, and the basement of the church was opened for Midnight Mass on Christmas 1929. Built on Centre Street at the corner of the West Roxbury Parkway, the upper church was designed as a Romanesque church by the noted architect Edward T.P. Graham, and was completed in 1939. The church was so named because of the well-known interest in the Holy Name Society by Reverend William P. McNamara, the first rector of the new parish. (Courtesy of the West Roxbury Historical Society.)

Fred and Dolores Agri Giannelli were married on October 14, 1956, at Holy Name Church. The dome in the main sanctuary of the church is a replica of that in Saint Clement's in Rome, the former titular church of the late William Cardinal O'Connell. (Courtesy of the Sammarco Family.)

Monsignor Charles Finn sits in the seat of a backhoe at the groundbreaking for the Holy Name School in 1953. The Brown Estate was acquired in 1935 and became known as "Holy Name Hill" after the school was built. (Courtesy of the BPL.)

The West Roxbury Catholic Women's Club was composed of women who belonged to Saint Theresa's Church and Holy Name Church. To raise money for their worthy causes, members of the club often performed in musicals and minstrels, such as this theatrical performance in 1949. (Courtesy of the West Roxbury Historical Society.)

Four
The Attraction

The attraction of living in West Roxbury was obvious to most people in the late nineteenth century. West Roxbury offered a country setting with grazing cows near newly laid out streets and all the charms of small town living, while being accessible to Boston via streetcars on the West Roxbury and Roslindale Street Railway and the trains of the Boston and Providence Railroad. Here, cows graze in a field near a haystack in West Roxbury about 1885. (Courtesy of the West Roxbury Historical Society.)

A group of friends enjoy an outing in West Roxbury in the late nineteenth century. (Courtesy of the West Roxbury Historical Society.)

Newly laid out streets bisected farms such as Mill Hill in West Roxbury at the turn of the century. The advance of progress is evident by the presence of a telephone pole on the right.

William S. Mitchell was a contractor and builder in West Roxbury at the turn of the century. It was said of his contracting firm that it "has built one hundred or more houses in West Roxbury, Newton and Jamaica Plain." (Courtesy of the West Roxbury Historical Society.)

William Mitchell built his home at 33 Farrington Street in West Roxbury. A commodious Stick-style house, it had a carriage house on the right. After he moved to West Roxbury in 1873, Mitchell was initially the foreman of the Anawan Land Company before he started his own contracting business. (Courtesy of the West Roxbury Historical Society.)

A vacant lot at what would eventually be the Everett family's home at 107 Temple Street shows how fast the development of West Roxbury took place in the late nineteenth century. On the left is the Osgood House at 99 Temple Street, and on the right the Spear House at 115 Temple Street. Notice the wood planks serving as sidewalks. (Courtesy of the West Roxbury Historical Society.)

Hemlock Gorge was photographed in 1899 with the surging waters of the Charles River passing under a high stone bridge. (Courtesy of the West Roxbury Historical Society.)

Another attraction of living in West Roxbury was the vast amount of open land. Here residents attend a baseball game at Spear Field (now Billings Field) at the turn of the century. (Courtesy of the West Roxbury Historical Society.)

Reverend John Carroll Poland lived at 124 Temple Street. An Episcopalian minister, he saw that the rapid development of West Roxbury after its annexation to Boston in 1874 was not only a historic event, but that the evolving history of the community needed to be preserved. Reverend Poland established the West Roxbury Historical Society in 1931. (Courtesy of the West Roxbury Historical Society.)

Stores such as those at the Gordon Block on Spring Street were within walking distance of the new homes being built, as were many convenient railroad depots. These conveniences and others gave residents many reasons to live in West Roxbury. (Courtesy of the West Roxbury Historical Society.)

Gordon Hall was an impressive Colonial Revival block at the corner of Summer and Spring Streets. Notice the impressive broken arch pediments above the entrances and the billboard advertisements for Ivorine, a washing powder. (Courtesy of the West Roxbury Historical Society.)

Herbert L. Baker built his home on a vast tract of land at 308 Bellevue Street. An attorney, Baker was also a state senator serving as chairman of Bills in the Third Reading and a member of the Judiciary Committee and the Committee on Woman Suffrage (voting, that is!). (Courtesy of the West Roxbury Historical Society.)

William H. Bowdlear lived at 16 Pelton Street in West Roxbury. A manufacturer of wax for the trade, he had an extensive plant for the refining and manufacture of wax in Williamsville. (Courtesy of the West Roxbury Historical Society.)

Park Street was laid out in 1849 and connects Mountford Street and Woodard Road. By the early twentieth century, it had been built up with comfortable houses.

Streetcars were photographed at the junction of Washington and Grove Streets in the Germantown section of West Roxbury in the 1920s. (Courtesy of the West Roxbury Historical Society.)

Junction of Grove & Washington Sts.,
W. Roxbury, Mass.

At the turn of the century, the junction of Washington and Grove Streets was a country crossroad. Known as Germantown for the large number of Germans living in the area, it was largely developed in the early to mid-twentieth century. The streetcar is a semi-convertible and is traveling south to the towns of Dedham, Norwood, and East Walpole. (Courtesy of the West Roxbury Historical Society.)

Washington Street was originally laid out as the Dedham Turnpike in 1805, and connected Boston and towns to the south. Named after General George Washington, it became a busy thoroughfare connecting Boston and Dedham. Notice the large outcropping of Roxbury puddingstone on the right, and the gas lamps that were removed in 1931. (Courtesy of David Rooney.)

Centre Street, seen in 1932 just south of Mount Vernon Street, was laid out in 1662 as the Middlepost Road, connecting Boston and Hartford, Connecticut. Renamed Centre Street, it was literally in the center of the western section of Roxbury known as Spring Street. On the left can be seen the West Roxbury Congregational Church. (Courtesy of David Rooney.)

Centre Street, seen from the corner of Hastings Street, has been a thriving shopping area since the late nineteenth century. Delivery trucks and automobiles are parked along the street while deliveries are being made and shoppers procure goods. The spire of the Theodore Parker Church can be seen on the left.

Five

Schools

The first and second classes of the Mount Vernon Street School posed for a class portrait on the porch of the school in the spring of 1890. Their teachers were Miss Emily R. Porter and Mr. John C. Ryder, who are standing first and fourth, from the left, in the rear row. (Courtesy of the West Roxbury Historical Society.)

The first schoolhouse in West Roxbury was opened in 1767, on land donated by Jeremiah Richards, who "in consideration of my good will and respect, to the proprietors and inhabitants of the westerly end of Roxbury . . . to have and to hold for the use of a school . . . and to their heirs behoof forever." The old Baker Street School was a typical one-room primary school that was built in 1855 and used until 1935, when it was closed. (Courtesy of David Rooney.)

Westerly Hall was both a primary school (on the second floor) and the West Roxbury Free Library (on the first floor). Located on Centre Street, on the present site of the library, these students pose for a class portrait on May 10, 1878. (Courtesy of the West Roxbury Historical Society.)

Standing on the steps of Westerly Hall are students of the class of 1891. Westerly Hall was a two-story wood-framed building embellished with corner quoining and a bracketed frontal gable. When the present library was built in 1922, Westerly Hall was moved across the street and was used by the American Legion. (Courtesy of the West Roxbury Historical Society.)

Posing for a class portrait are Westerly Hall Primary School students in 1901. Their teacher is in the back row on the right. (Courtesy of the West Roxbury Historical Society.)

The Mount Vernon Street Primary School was a two-story schoolhouse with a mansard roof that was built in 1862. Mr. Abner J. Nutter was the first headmaster of the school, and was succeeded in 1888 by John C. Ryder. (Courtesy of the West Roxbury Historical Society.)

Students of the Mount Vernon Street School pose for a class portrait in February of 1895. (Courtesy of the West Roxbury Historical Society.)

Class one of the Mount Vernon Street Grammar School posed for their class portrait in the spring of 1891. Their teacher, Mr. William E.C. Rich, is in the back row, third from the left. (Courtesy of the West Roxbury Historical Society.)

Students of class one of the Mount Vernon Street School pose with two of their teachers after a baseball game. (Courtesy of the West Roxbury Historical Society.)

The second school building of the Robert Gould Shaw School was built in 1919 on Mount Vernon Street, and was designed by the Boston architectural firm of Blackall, Clapp & Whittemore.

Colonel Robert Gould Shaw (1837–1863) commanded the 54th Massachusetts Infantry, a company that was composed solely of black soldiers. Born and raised in West Roxbury, Shaw was an abolitionist who led the first black regiment to serve in the war and was immensely, and justifiably, proud of his men. He was killed in an attack on Fort Wagner, along with 255 of his soldiers.

Students of class one of the Robert Gould Shaw School pose in the Master's Room in 1895. Mr. William E.C. Rich, the headmaster, and Miss Emily R. Porter stand near the blackboard. (Courtesy of the West Roxbury Historical Society.)

Abner J. Nutter (1822–1911) is shown in retirement after having served as master of West Roxbury Schools from 1857 to 1888. He sits in a rocking chair that was presented to him on his 80th birthday from friends and neighbors. (Courtesy of the West Roxbury Historical Society.)

The Vane School was a brick schoolhouse with distinctive Flemish stepped gables.

Sir Henry Vane (1612–1662) was governor of the Massachusetts Bay Colony from 1636 to 1637, and was knighted by Charles I in 1640. He was beheaded in London in 1662 for his opposition to the Crown.

Students of the Hewins School on Emmons Road performed Shakespeare's *As You Like It* in 1916. The cast included the following, from left to right: (seated) Helen Geromanos and an unidentified young lady; (kneeling) Betty Gibson, Katherine Gallagher, Frances Allen, Lucy Allen, Eleanor Grover, Helga Lundin, Rachel Foster, Betty Gibbs, Eleanore Haigh, Caroline Foster, Katherine Gibson, and Frances Tyler; (standing) Lucy Worthington, Katherine Tracey, Betsy Allen, two unidentified students, Margaret Kemp, Muriel Robinson, Olive Bogart, Frances Tilton, an unidentified student, Helen Estabrook, and Mary McLaughlin. (Courtesy of the West Roxbury Historical Society.)

The Sophia W. Ripley School was built in 1932 on Temple Street, and was designed by architect Harold R. Duffie. Sophia Warren Dana Ripley (1803–1861) was the wife of Reverend George Ripley and was one of the founders of the Brook Farm Institute of Agriculture and Education in West Roxbury. She was an early, and ardent, feminist and wrote for *The Dial*. The school was closed in 1981 and demolished in 1984. (Courtesy of David Rooney.)

The Roxbury Latin School was founded in 1635 by Reverend John Eliot, minister of the Roxbury Meeting House. The school moved to West Roxbury in 1922, after the Codman Estate on Centre Street and Cottage Avenue (now Saint Theresa Road) was purchased. The Georgian Revival campus was designed by the architectural firm of Perry, Shaw and Hepburn.

Students of the Roxbury Latin School leave Gordon Hall in June 1945.

The Parental School for Truants was established in 1892 as a reformatory institution in West Roxbury. The school was on the former grounds of the Bolles Estate, and had a complex of buildings on what is now the site of the Veterans Administration Hospital at the junction of Spring Street and the Veterans of Foreign Wars Parkway. A group of the uniformed pupils stands in front of the school at the turn of the century.

M.J. Perkins was the superintendent of the Parental School for Truants at the turn of the century. During his tenure, an average year would have about 150 boys committed to the school and 50 discharged from it.

The Reading Room at the Parental School for Truants was a pleasant and well-furnished room for the boys to study in.

The Cottage at the Parental School was a three-story dormitory with a master who presided over the house. The master took his meals with the boys in the common dining room and also acted as an adult role model for the boys to, hopefully, emulate. The school became an army hospital during World War I, and a hospital for disabled veterans before the Veterans Administration Hospital was built in 1944.

Six

A Streetcar Suburb

Mr. and Mrs. Arthur Hoyt of 25 Ivory Street represent the quintessential streetcar suburb residents of Boston in the late nineteenth century. They were photographed in their fashionable horse-drawn carriage, he with a silk top hat and she with a fashionable bonnet, with examples of the new houses being built on Temple, Ivory, Perham, and Dent Streets rising in the background. (Courtesy of the West Roxbury Historical Society.)

The Attwood House was built at 78 Bellevue Street, and was photographed about 1885. The Attwood children stand on the piazza and walkway in front of the house, which was considerably enlarged in the late 1880s. (Courtesy of the West Roxbury Historical Society.)

The Walker House was built in 1866 at the corner of Centre and Mount Vernon Streets. Lydia Walker stands in front of the house with her son. (Courtesy of the West Roxbury Historical Society.)

The Kendrick family, complete with their horse and carriage, stands in front of their house at 52 Dent Street, about 1880. (Courtesy of the West Roxbury Historical Society.)

The Poland family poses on the side porch and front lawn of their home at 144 Temple Street. From left to right are: (on the porch) Helen, Belle, and Grandmother Poland; (on the lawn) Everett and Edward F. Poland. (Courtesy of the West Roxbury Historical Society.)

This Queen Anne extravaganza epitomized the houses that were being built in West Roxbury in the late nineteenth century. A piazza wraps around the front of the house and an octagonal bay is capped with a conical roof. The turret has an observatory at the top, and the house is sheathed in fanciful shingles. Mother holds Gretchen on the piazza; Robert (right) and Lionel are on the lawn. (Courtesy of the West Roxbury Historical Society.)

Standing on the lawn at the corner of Ivory and Temple Streets are, from left to right: Mrs. Dyer Kendrick, Mr. Dyer Kendrick, Miss Kendrick, an unidentified individual, and Mr. and Mrs. Arthur Hoyt. The house is a Shingle-style house, with a Romanesque Revival wood-shingle arched entrance porch. It also has a gambrel-facaded gable with a palladian window, that is partially obscured by the tree. (Courtesy of the West Roxbury Historical Society.)

The Jordan House was built at 137 Mount Vernon Street and was photographed in 1900. On the left is the Snelling House, a Colonial Revival house, which stands in marked contrast to the Victorian style of the Jordan House. (Courtesy of the West Roxbury Historical Society.)

After Morse's Field was subdivided and Temple Street was laid out, it was built up with houses such as 107 Temple Street (the Everett House) on the left and 109 Temple Street (the Watters House) on the right. (Courtesy of the West Roxbury Historical Society.)

The estate of Jason S. Bailey was at 200 Corey Street, and was a magnificent Shingle-style mansion set on extensive grounds

The entrance to the Bailey Mansion had rustic granite piers supporting a balcony, and a massive turret with fanciful peaked dormers projecting from the roof. (Courtesy of the West Roxbury Historical Society.)

Seen from the lawn, the Bailey Mansion was undoubtedly the grandest house ever built in West Roxbury. The carriage house and stables were on the far right. (Courtesy of the West Roxbury Historical Society.)

On the Bailey Estate, opposite the Lily Pond, were a conservatory and greenhouses, where plants were grown for bedding specimens that provided colorful flowers all season long. (Courtesy of the West Roxbury Historical Society.)

Mr. and Mrs. B.J. Johnson and their daughter Elizabeth pose in their 1912 Hupmobile near the old Colburn House on Centre Street. The Johnsons lived at 2144 Centre Street in West Roxbury and "Teddy," who sits on the hood of the automobile, shared Elizabeth's room. (Courtesy of the West Roxbury Historical Society.)

Harry L. Whittemore lived at 1977 Centre Street, in a fashionable Colonial Revival house. Whittemore was in the milk trade and had a thriving delivery route throughout West Roxbury, Roslindale, and Jamaica Plain. (Courtesy of the West Roxbury Historical Society.)

Danville Street connects Bellevue and Wren Street and was laid out in the 1890s. (Courtesy of David Rooney.)

Hastings Street connects Montview Street and the tracks of the old Boston and Providence Railroad, and was laid out in 1886 with large Colonial Revival houses. (Courtesy of David Rooney.)

Maple Street connects Centre Street and the Veterans of Foreign Wars Parkway.

Maxfield Street was an unpaved road at the turn of the century and connected La Grange and Bellevue Streets.

Meredith Street connects Kenneth Street and Clement Avenue. An open "horseless carriage" passes by the street in 1904.

A mother and child walk down Park Street, just past Centre Street, at the turn of the century. The unpaved street is rutted with the marks of carriage wheels and a horse-drawn delivery wagon approaches. (Courtesy of David Rooney.)

Stratford Street connects Clement Avenue and Bellevue Hill Road. Laid out with shade trees and wide lawns, the street gives the impression of a comfortable neighborhood from the turn of the century.

The Everett family lived at 238 Vermont Street in this Colonial Revival house.

Seven

The Town, Police, and Fire Departments

A horse-drawn fire engine is shown here on Centre Street about 1885. These engines used chemicals to extinguish fires, rather than the water used in pumper engines. The firemen, complete with helmets, pose on a hook and ladder truck as their faithful mascot rests beside them. (Courtesy of the West Roxbury Historical Society.)

A formal portrait of the West Roxbury Fire Department about 1885 shows them just outside the doors of the firehouse on Center Street. (Courtesy of the West Roxbury Historical Society.)

Peter F. Gateley (1854–1936) lived at 480 La Grange Street, and was photographed in 1889 while a member of the West Roxbury Fire Department. Gateley retired in 1926 with just over forty years of dedicated service. (Courtesy of the West Roxbury Historical Society.)

Members of the West Roxbury Fire Department pose outside the new brick firehouse on Centre Street which was designed in 1898 by John A. Fox. With massive arched doors and prominent brownstone rustication and quoining, the firehouse was as impressive as it was necessary. (Courtesy of the West Roxbury Historical Society.)

The captain of the West Roxbury Fire Department sits in front of the firehouse on Centre Street in 1905. His crew provided prompt assistance when the fire alarm sounded, at all hours of the day or night. (Courtesy of the West Roxbury Historical Society.)

The West Roxbury Police Station was located in the old Highland Club House after a new clubhouse was built across the street at the corner of Centre and Corey Streets. A squad of policemen file out of the station, heading toward Hastings Street about 1910. (Courtesy of the West Roxbury Historical Society.)

Officer Edward R. Tilton and his mount pose at the Spring Street grade crossing about 1898. On the left is John J. Kane's Horseshoeing Shop, and on the right is Whipple & Company Coal and Wood. (Courtesy of the West Roxbury Historical Society.)

A group of West Roxbury residents pose for their photograph on Election Day in 1906. They are inside the voting booth that was set up in the school yard of the Mount Vernon Street School. (Courtesy of the West Roxbury Historical Society.)

Fast Day was held at Speare Field (now Billings Field) on La Grange Street on April 7, 1887. These "Fast Days" were the Ember days of Spring. Participating in the bicycle race were, from left to right: (kneeling on the left) Dexter Chamberlain, Walter Kingman, and Fred Long; (behind them) an unidentified man, Charles Earnshaw, George Bennett, Edward Rollins, Levi Willcutt, Howard Gates (on the bicycle), Eliot Dennett (on the bicycle), an unidentified man, Ned Wade, Everett Westcott, and Edward Prescott. (Courtesy of the West Roxbury Historical Society.)

Joseph H. Billings, for whom Billings Field was named, was the proprietor of the Billings Sheepskin Factory, at the corner of Centre and La Grange Streets. It was said of him that he "was intensely fond of his land, his well-bred horses, oxen and cows. He had thirty-five acres of land, made beautiful with trees and shrubs, fruit trees and grass, and some used to say Joe [Billings] would cover it every year with dollars." (Courtesy of the BPL.)

A team of young baseball players pose on Billings Field after a game in 1929. During the winter months Billings Field was often flooded for skating. (Courtesy of the West Roxbury Historical Society.)

Eight

West Roxbury Businesses

Charlie Kelley delivered ice by wagon in West Roxbury at the turn of the century. The West Roxbury Ice Company would "harvest" ice at Cow Island Pond and store the blocks in an ice house, on what is now the site of the MDC skating rink. Kelley, holding a pair of ice tongs, was photographed at the corner of Temple and Ivory Streets while on his rounds to replenish melted ice blocks in neighborhood "iceboxes." (Courtesy of the West Roxbury Historical Society.)

A group of workers of John McCormack's Blacksmith and Woodworking Shop pose with a grill from an automobile that is being serviced. McCormack's Shop provided for the general repair of truck bodies and shoed horses as well! (Courtesy of the West Roxbury Historical Society.)

Consumer's Oil Company was operated by John V. Kenney. Here, one of the delivery trucks is parked at a gas station at Centre Street and West Roxbury Parkway, where the police station is presently located. Photographed in 1930, the Brown House, now the site of the Holy Name School, can be seen in the background on the hill often referred to as "Holy Name Hill." (Courtesy of the West Roxbury Historical Society.)

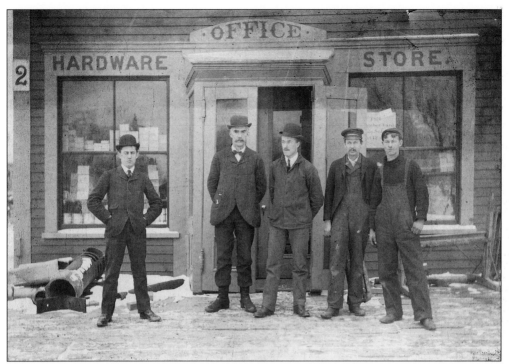

Standing in front of the W.T. McLaughlin & Company office and hardware store in 1895 are, from left to right: Guy Mitchell, John Galligan, Charles Locke, ? Borden, and ? Terhune. (Courtesy of the West Roxbury Historical Society.)

At the corners of Centre and La Grange Streets in 1875 were the G.A. Newhall & Company grocery store and the Billings Sheepskin Factory. (Courtesy of the West Roxbury Historical Society.)

The Billings Sheepskin Factory was owned and operated by Joseph H. Billings. It was built as a leather dressing factory and was later was used as Robinson's Dye House. A horse-drawn delivery wagon awaits a bale of leather hides from the shipping door. (Courtesy of the West Roxbury Historical Society.)

Workers at the Billings Sheepskin Factory stand on the La Grange Street side of the factory about 1880. The factory, then used as Robinson's Dye House, burned to the ground on March 4, 1891. (Courtesy of the West Roxbury Historical Society.)

The Brookline Pumping Station was located on the banks of the Charles River, in a red brick Romanesque Revival waterworks building. (Courtesy of the West Roxbury Historical Society.)

Workers of the Brookline Pumping Station "relax" over a game of cards in the boiler room about 1900. The chairman of this "committee meeting" was Henry G. Young, and he was obviously the "perfect host," judging by the large number of shot glasses on the card table. (Courtesy of the West Roxbury Historical Society.)

M.T. Mullen had a market and fish market on Centre Street in West Roxbury at the turn of the century. On the far right are George Feeney and ? Morrissey. (Courtesy of the West Roxbury Historical Society.)

Louis Vogel & Company was the purveyor of Providence Brewing Company's Lager Beer and Alley's East India Stock Ale. Vogel, standing in the door, had his store at the corner of Washington and Grove Streets in Germantown. (Courtesy of the West Roxbury Historical Society.)

This motorized hearse of Stokes' Funeral Parlor was the first of its kind in West Roxbury. (Courtesy of the West Roxbury Historical Society.)

Waldo J. Stokes was an undertaker at 1896 Centre Street in West Roxbury. It was said that he was "prepared to do the highest grade of funeral directing," and did a large and thriving business.

Pierce's Block was located at 1870 and 1876 Centre Street, and housed the pharmacy of Jennie H. Sumner, the dental office of Dr. Frank D. Pierce (who built the block), and the tailor shop of H. Greenblat. On the far left can be seen the Highland Club House at Corey Street. Today, David's Books is located today in the right-hand storefront; Images Salon is on the left. (Courtesy of the West Roxbury Historical Society.)

The Boston Trailer Park was laid out on Route 1 on the site of Caledonian Grove, an open area that was used for recreation at the turn of the century. Owners Chet and Mrs. Ader were members of the New England Mobile Home Association and offered parking spaces for one's trailer that provided "Sewer Connections . . . Tiled Showers . . . Automatic Laundry," or almost all the comforts of home on the banks of the Charles River! This is the only trailer park in the city of Boston.

Nine
Mount Bellevue

This turn-of-the-century photograph was taken looking south on La Grange Street from Shaw Street toward Mount Bellevue. The water tower that surmounted the hill can be glimpsed through the trees. La Grange Street, which connects Washington Street and Hammond Pond Parkway in Brookline, was laid out in 1849 and was named after the estate of the Marquis de Lafayette, a hero of the American Revolution and a French nobleman. The crest of the hill was donated to the city of Boston by William G. Blakemore as a park. (Courtesy of the West Roxbury Historical Society.)

This wood shingled Romanesque Revival water tower, built in 1888, had a shaft in the center that would store water for periods of drought. An enclosed staircase on the right led to an observatory, which was the highest elevation in Boston, and afforded unsurpassed views of Boston and the countryside.

A view looking east from the Mount Bellevue water tower shows open land that descended toward Roslindale. (Courtesy of the West Roxbury Historical Society.)

102

Looking toward Centre Street from the Mount Bellevue water tower, the spire of the Second Church in Roxbury at the corner of Centre and Church Streets can be seen in the center. Roslindale is on the right, and West Roxbury Village is on the left.

Looking west from the Mount Bellevue water tower, the hills of Dedham and Newton can be seen in the distance. The Robert Gould Shaw School can be seen in the center of the photograph.

Another panoramic view, taken in 1890 from the Mount Bellevue water tower, shows the impressive and breathtaking vistas that could be seen from the highest elevation in the city of Boston. The hill was acquired from the city by the Metropolitan Park Commission in 1894.

The wood shingled water tower was replaced by a granite block storage tank, which, though water tight and solid looking, was architecturally uninteresting and would eventually be obscured by trees planted during the 1930s. Today, Mount Bellevue is covered by a dense forest of trees, and though it has remained undeveloped, it no longer affords the spectacular views of a century ago.

Ten
Transportation

A horse and carriage waits at the entrance to the Highland station of the Boston and Providence Railroad line in West Roxbury. The train station was designed as a step-gabled structure of stone, with sloping slate roofs. The line served passenger stations in Roslindale Village, Highland, West Roxbury Village, and Spring Street before arriving at Dedham. Along the railroad line, both residences and small businesses were built, creating a neighborhood that grew rapidly throughout the nineteenth century. (Courtesy of the BPL.)

The Dedham branch of the Boston and Providence Railroad was opened in 1851, and the Highland station was photographed about 1890. The Highland station was built on land donated by Andrew S. March, for whom March Avenue, Terrace, and Way were named. On the far left was the barn of the Mann Farm. The farm was eventually laid out as Stratford, Meredith, and Kenneth Streets, and Clement Avenue. (Courtesy of the West Roxbury Historical Society.)

A conductor and two passengers stand on the platform of the West Roxbury Village depot. The photograph was taken prior to 1898, for after that date the grade crossing was done away with. (Courtesy of the West Roxbury Historical Society.)

The West Roxbury Village depot was just past the crossing at La Grange Street. The gate tender for the railroad, Thomas McIntosh, lived in the house on the right. In the distance can be seen the spire of the West Roxbury Congregational Church. (Courtesy of the West Roxbury Historical Society.)

The grade crossing at the West Roxbury depot, looking across the tracks toward Centre Street, was photographed before 1898. On the left is Chapin Avenue and on the right is Dent Street (originally known as Jordan Street). (Courtesy of the West Roxbury Historical Society.)

The "Needham Local" steams along tracks that were depressed under Centre Street. The spire of the West Roxbury Congregational Church looms above the stone wall. (Courtesy of the West Roxbury Historical Society.)

Gordon Hall, a commercial block at the junction of Summer, Powell, and Spring Streets, was adjacent to Spring Street. Spring Street was being depressed for the railroad. (Courtesy of the West Roxbury Historical Society.)

Spring Street, about where Aleric Street joins Spring Street, was being excavated here in 1898. The grade was being changed for the bridge at the station. On the left is the Whelan House, and a passenger train can be seen in the distance. (Courtesy of the West Roxbury Historical Society.)

West Roxbury Station was at La Grange and Dent Streets, and was above grade after 1898, when La Grange Street was depressed under the railroad bridge. (Courtesy of Claude Mac Gray.)

Centre Street, in West Roxbury Village at the corner of Hastings Street, was traversed by streetcar tracks by 1856, when a horse-drawn streetcar line connected West Roxbury to Dudley Street in Roxbury. This 1939 photograph shows a streetcar approaching from the east, the stores along Centre Street, and the spire of the Theodore Parker Church. (Courtesy of David Rooney.)

The West Roxbury and Roslindale Street Railway had streetcars that would often be rented for afternoon outings. A group of gentlemen arrive in 1898 at Westwood Park in a special car, #38. (Courtesy of the West Roxbury Historical Society.)

The streetcars of the West Roxbury and Roslindale Street Railway brought increased development to the towns in the late nineteenth century. Houses would spring up as if by magic to meet the need for new residents of the "streetcar suburbs." (Courtesy of the BPL.)

A streetcar approaches the junction of Spring and Centre Streets in 1904. (Courtesy of David Rooney.)

A "Duplex Car" was added to the West Roxbury and Roslindale Street Railway, connecting Forest Hills on the Elevated Railway to Oakdale Square. George Whittemore is the motorman, and Edward Vollert is the conductor in this *c.* 1898 photograph. (Courtesy of the West Roxbury Historical Society.)

A streetcar heads west on Washington Street, near Grove Street, in 1937. The two-family house on the left had recently been built but the rest of the street remains fairly undeveloped. (Courtesy of David Rooney.)

Eleven

Clubbin' Around Town

The "Midgets' Wedding" was performed by neighborhood children in the hall of the Highland Club of West Roxbury in 1907. Highland Hall would be the setting for numerous neighborhood events and meetings, including those of the West Roxbury Sinfonietta, the West Roxbury Citizens' Association, the West Roxbury Woman's Club, Morning Musicales, and the dancing classes of Miss Widmer. (Courtesy of the West Roxbury Historical Society.)

The clubhouse of the Highland Club was originally at the corner of Centre and Hastings Streets. An interesting Shingle-style building, it later became the West Roxbury Police Station. Notice the open land in the rear! (Courtesy of the West Roxbury Historical Society.)

Members of the Highland Club would often perform minstrels, theatricals, and musicals in the hall. A cast, and the musicians, posed on the stage at the turn of the century. (Courtesy of the West Roxbury Historical Society.)

The Highland Club had a new clubhouse built at the corner of Centre and Corey Streets in 1901. An impressive Colonial Revival clubhouse, with Ionic columns supporting a dentilled pediment, it was demolished in 1965. An office building was built on the site.

Moseley's on the Charles was a popular banquet hall that could be rented for weddings, anniversaries, and dances. The Spring Street Canoe House, with the canoe launches, is beside the club. (Courtesy of the West Roxbury Historical Society.)

Members of the Arcadian Outing Club pose in Pipping's Grove on September 27, 1903. The members, with their dogs and a caged parrot, look quite content. (Courtesy of the West Roxbury Historical Society.)

Brandishing a carving knife and sharpening file, a chef-hatted member of the Arcadian Club sits behind a caged parrot, whose wings are all aflutter! (Courtesy of the West Roxbury Historical Society.)

A "May Party" was given in 1913 by Mrs. Edward A. Rollins, a music teacher who lived at 8 Rutledge Street in West Roxbury. From left to right are: (front row) Francis Mahady, Mabel Crockett, unidentified, Ruth McLean, Mary McLaughlin, Betty Gibbs, Rachel Foster, Marnie Fickett, unidentified, and unidentified; (middle row) Betty Gibson, Connie Kingman, Elizabeth McLean, Caroline Foster, Katherine Gibson, unidentified, Dorothy Swan, unidentified, Stephen Palmer, Charlotte Smith (who was Queen of the May), Edgar Deming, Marion Kendrick, Elizabeth Fowler, Eleanore Haigh, unidentified, unidentified, Davis Mahady, and Janet Warren; (back row) Margaret Kemp, Frances Smith, Frances Warren, Mildred McCormack, Lois Curtis, Betty Foster, Lorena Kennedy, Teddy Slack, Winas Gibson, unidentified, unidentified, Beatrice Haigh, Mary Foster, and Christine Howard. (Courtesy of the West Roxbury Historical Society.)

The West Roxbury Post 167 of the American Legion poses proudly. From left to right are: (seated) Ralph Dudley, Bill Benson, Ed Johnson, Tom Sheehan, John Dervan, unidentified, Charles O'Connell, and Bill O'Brien; (middle row) Bill Sullivan, Bill Nagle, Claus Meyer, unidentified, Gregory Prior, Al Perkins, Tony Connetta (leader), Frank Jackson, Dr. McCarthy, Fred Mahoney, unidentified, unidentified, Bernie Hughes, and John Mahoney; (back row) Buck Welch, Lorne Thayer, unidentified, Al Kelte, unidentified, unidentified, and Charles Feeney. The rear two horns are Ray Keene and Hans Koppe. (Courtesy of the West Roxbury Historical Society.)

The West Roxbury Woman's Club sponsored a tour of gardens in West Roxbury to commemorate the tercentenary of the founding of Boston (1630–1930). In the garden of the General Cornelius G. Attwood House on Bellevue Street are Mrs. Harry Sutton and Mrs. William Little, members of the garden tour committee. (Courtesy of the West Roxbury Historical Society.)

The West Roxbury Woman's Club was organized in 1911. Its mission was "for the purpose of education, and encouraging in women united thought and action for service in the community." The club disbanded in 1993 after having served West Roxbury well for over eight decades. Few realize that the first district nurse in West Roxbury was secured in 1914 through the club's efforts. (Courtesy of the West Roxbury Historical Society.)

Twelve
Spring Street and the Samoset Canoe Club

Two friends pose in their canoe near the Vine Rock Bridge in 1899. The Vine Rock Bridge crossed the Charles River, and pedestrians can be seen leaning on the wood embankment. An ode to the Charles River penned by Henry Wadsworth Longfellow captures the feeling of the river: "River! that in silence windest, Through the meadows, bright and free, Till at length thy rest thou findest, In the bosom of the sea!"

A group of bathers stand on the launch watching canoeists on the Charles River in 1920. The Samoset Canoe Club's boathouse was situated across from the Olde Irish Ale House. The club raced against other clubs, such as the Night Owls, Breed's, Crescent, Omicron Delta, Dedham, and Needham Canoe Clubs. (Courtesy of the BPL.)

Shown here standing on the Vine Rock Bridge in 1921 are Bart Baird, Roland Graham, and Allan McIntosh. (Courtesy of the West Roxbury Historical Society.)

Bill Cox is shown making a "Jacknife Dive" in 1924 from a ladder on the canoe launch on the Charles River. (Courtesy of the West Roxbury Historical Society.)

People along the canoe launch in 1920 seek to rent a canoe for an enjoyable afternoon on the Charles River. After rowing for an hour or two, many tired canoeists would relax in one of the many restaurants near Spring Street such as the Waiting Room Spa, Gagliard's Cafe, or the Dew Drop Inn.

Posing with the Cassidy Trophy are members of the Samoset Canoe Club, who were the Eastern Division Champions in 1930. From left to right are: (front row) Shanning, Volk, the Cassidy Memorial Trophy, Coach Schmidt, and Amos; (back row) Bingham, Grauman, Volk, Zaboy, Volk, and Kunan. (Courtesy of the West Roxbury Historical Society.)

Rowing in a long canoe in 1930 was this lineup, from left to right: Volk, Grauman, Shanning, Volk, Kunan, Zaboy, Amos, Bingham, and Voke. (Courtesy of the West Roxbury Historical Society.)

Members of the Single Blade Club are shown here during the 1924 carnival and regatta of the Samoset Canoe Club on the Charles River. From left to right are: Weider, Herman, Moore, Florham, Farnum, Page, Daisy, and MacMillan. (Courtesy of the West Roxbury Historical Society.)

Racing in a single blade tandem in 1924 are Weider, Herman, Moore, and MacMillan. Most of the canoe races were over distances of five hundred yards, one mile, with some races lasting up to four miles. (Courtesy of the West Roxbury Historical Society.)

The Eastern Division Senior Tandem Blade Single Champions in 1930 were Volk and Zaboy.
(Courtesy of the West Roxbury Historical Society.)

James Michel Curley, mayor of Boston, presents the Point Trophy to members of the Samoset
Canoe Club in 1924. (Courtesy of the West Roxbury Historical Society.)

Thirteen

The Library

In 1922, a new building designed by local architect Mr. Oscar for the West Roxbury Branch of the Boston Public Library replaced Westerly Hall, which had served as both a library and a primary school. The first library in West Roxbury was the "Spring Street Social Library," which was initially kept at the store of Samuel Cookson, on Walter Street, and later at the home of Elizabeth Corey, on Centre Street. While the library was kept at the Corey House, "it was the custom of those wanting books to go in without knocking and help themselves, pausing generally for a social chat with Mrs. Corey." On the left is the West Roxbury Congregational Church, which was later demolished, allowing room for a modern addition to the library.

Miss Carrie L. Morse (1863–1962) had been the branch librarian in West Roxbury for fifty years when she retired in 1933. Photographed in front of the library upon her retirement, Miss Morse was also a noted local historian and a charter member of the West Roxbury Woman's Club. (Courtesy of the West Roxbury Historical Society.)

Members of the Summer Reading Club of the West Roxbury Library pose on the library steps in 1934. (Courtesy of the West Roxbury Historical Society.)

Young patrons of the West Roxbury Library pose for a photograph in 1934. (Courtesy of the West Roxbury Historical Society.)

It was a busy afternoon in April 1956 in the Children's Reading Room of the West Roxbury Library. (Courtesy of the West Roxbury Historical Society.)

Acknowledgments

I would like to extend my sincere thanks to Bob Murphy of the West Roxbury Historical Society for his assistance in researching this book, for without his help and interest it would not have been possible. The majority of the photographs used in this book came from the archives of the West Roxbury Historical Society. Housed in the Feeney Room in the West Roxbury Branch of the Boston Public Library, the archives and photograph collection have been meticulously categorized by an archive committee, to whom I am indebted.

I would also like to thank the following for their assistance in researching this book on West Roxbury, Massachusetts, and for their continued support and interest:

Daniel J. Ahlin, Anthony Bognanno, Lorna Palumbo Bognanno, president of the West Roxbury-Roslindale Rotary, Paul and Helen Graham Buchanan, Richard Bunbury, Jamie Carter, Jeanne Clancy, Lillian Crowley, the late Marie Crowley, Dexter, Miriam Dickey, Marion Ego, Fred and Dolores Agri Giannelli, Edward W. Gordon, David Gorin of David's Books, Elizabeth Doris-Gustin, president of the West Roxbury Historical Society, Christopher Keneally, James Z. Kyprianos, Claude Mac Gray, Barbara Martin, Edward McGowan, the late Carrie L. Morse, Robert Murphy, David Noyd, Reverend Claudius Nowinski, Marilyn Oberle, Marjorie O'Neill, Linda Ozier, Stephen and Susan Paine, Reverend Michael Parise, William Reid, David Rooney, Dennis Ryan, Anthony and Mary Mitchell Sammarco, Rosemary Sammarco, Sylvia Sandeen, Robert Bayard Severy, William Varrell, Shirley Walsh, the West Roxbury Historical Society, Virginia White, and Catherine Coyne, Branch Librarian, and the staff of the West Roxbury Branch of the Boston Public Library.